The Danger
of the
Safe Place

Andre Boggerty

DEDICATION

This book is dedicated to Fear.

I beat you!

ACKNOWLEDGMENTS

It goes without saying that I would like to thank God and my Lord and Savior Jesus Christ! I am a product of Grace!

To my wife, Kim, thank you for taking this journey for over 20 years.

To my children Latuan, Shekinah, and Nadeem, thank you for letting me be your father. D'Andre and Sierra, I love you both!

Mom, words will fail to express my love and gratefulness for you! Dad, ours is a testimony of forgiveness and healing! Love you man! Earl, thanks for your calming presence! Mom Brenda, I love you and thank you for praying! Mom and Pop Bordley, I love you both more than you know.

My Brothers and Sisters, Dominique, John (RIP), William, Jalen, Rachel, Kenneacka, Diane and Lil' Diane, I am so glad God saw fit to unite us! Tamika, what else is there to say but I love you! John and Yvette, thanks for accepting me as your brother. Trina and Kim, thanks for allowing me to share your parents as my own.

My Grandmothers, thank you for taking me to church in my youth.

My Pastors, Anthony and Margo Wallace, thank you for tolerating and teaching me. I am not ashamed to say that everything God allows me to accomplish is a direct result of your impact in my life.

Apostles Tom and Angela Frederick, thank you for ministering to Kim and me. You are forever in my heart.

To all the men who have served as my mentors and role models, thank you! Special shout out to James Cagle, Lloyd

Wheatley and Steve Askew! You stayed with me when I did not deserve it! Lloyd, thank you for contributing your story to this book.

My Brothers Juan, Randy and Kamau, I cannot wait until we get together again!

To Kameka, Kim, Kenya, Kiesha and Sade, thanks for the years of friendship and encouragement!

Dr. Ernest Davis and Pastors Mason & Kim McGill, thank you for your wisdom over the years.

Ray Ramsey thank you for the insights you continue to provide and for agreeing to write the foreword.

My Crossroad Christian Church family thanks for loving your boy!

To the greatest fraternity ever established, Omega Psi Phi Fraternity, Inc. and my Line Brothers GP and Wes, thank you for making me a better man. The Brothers of Psi Iota Chapter!

Denise Barnes thank you for your wisdom!

To my editor Sonya McCray, thank you for your motivation and guidance with this book.

I am sure I missed some of you, but I got y'all in the next one!

Finally, to each of you who took the time to purchase and read this book, I pray it serves as motivation to leave your Safe Place and accomplish everything God has for you!

The Danger of the Safe Place

The Danger of the Safe Place

FOREWORD

We have all experienced that gut-wrenching feeling of regret that immediately grips us after missing a *moment*—an opportunity that could have changed our life for the better.

Whether our inability to take action was the result of a fear of failure, a fear of success, or a fear of making the wrong decision, in the end we decided the best way to respond to the opportunity was to play it safe. Like missing an exit on the highway, these missed opportunities may at the very least cost us precious time, energy, or other resources. At worst, these "exits" may never come around the same way again. For this reason, many profound books have been written, passionate talks have been given, and powerful quotes have been offered on the power of taking action.

Many leaders have focused their attention on the *rewards* of audacious action; however, few have highlighted the *dangers* of staying put, making this book both unique and important.

Andre teaches all who have weathered perpetual seasons of drought, journeyed through the wilderness of desperation, or wandered into the labyrinths of obscurity, anonymity, or ambiguity to respond by taking bolder and more frequent risks. Therefore, many of us continually reap the fruits of mediocrity because we continue to sow our God-inspired seeds of greatness into the barren fields of our comfort zones.

With this in mind, Andre systematically deconstructs the problem of safety and show us how it hinders us from God's best outcomes and ideal purposes for our life. He also dismantles our belief that we can remain where we are *spiritually* and move forward in healthy ways. We cannot just read, study, attend lectures, or dream up new ideas for ourselves, our businesses, or our families. If we are going to see real and lasting change, we must take an honest look at our need for comfort, and that transformation process begins with page one of *The Danger of the Safe Place*.

-*Pastor Raymond Ramsey*

CONTENTS

Introduction

In the Bible, God successfully used individuals who were willing to leave their Safe Place. My studies revealed that those who could not shift appropriately were left out or even died with unfulfilled purpose. Some, like Jonah, could not fathom leaving a Safe Place and suffered grave consequences until he or she obeyed. Yet, when Jonah finally listened to God and moved appropriately, an entire nation was saved. What about Saul and the Israelites who stayed camped in a valley because they were afraid to face the giant Goliath? Can you imagine the result if David never had found courage to show up for the fight?

Today the same principles apply. I recently had a choice to ultimately obey God. As a longtime believer, going with His lead should be a no-brainer, but how often does our faith waiver in the face of unfamiliarity? How many of us are unfulfilled, depressed, or impoverished -- both naturally and spiritually -- because we refuse to let go of a burning rope? God knows the other end of the rope is ablaze, but we wallow in its deceptive warmth and comforting appeal. We often question His voice and sit idly, tightly gripping our own understanding while oblivious to the dangers at hand. Many of us are treading water, doing our level best to simply survive in our current situations instead of using the same energy to shift and swim toward His promise.

How do you know when it is time to leave a Safe Place? Who, what, or where is your Safe Place? How do you leave and where do you go? The list of questions can go on and on, yet the answers may be simpler than you think. With this book, and the testimonies therein, I hope to provoke you to reconsider your current circumstances. Each chapter concludes with pertinent questions for reflection. Use them as an opportunity to challenge your present condition and begin the process of living your very best life.

At the conclusion of chapter five, you'll encounter the triumphant testimony of Lloyd Wheatley, a successful entrepreneur, author, and seasoned believer. His testimony is a clear example of how danger lurks when we disobey God in exchange for the notion of maintaining comfort. He now lives a full and rich life because of his willingness to avoid the safe places in his domain. His narrative is a clear example of how the promises of God are waiting just beyond our fears.

God's promises are not limited to financial prosperity, which is the lowest form of riches. Health, peace of mind, joy, and satisfaction among other attributes are not in your Safe Place; they must be obtained through obedience to His will. Your faith and corresponding works can transform your reality beyond your wildest dreams. These may sound like clichés, but do you believe? It's time to apply your faith in what He's specifically said to you and discover what Fear wants you to ignore.

The Danger of the Safe Place is like a jump start to a car, it may get a vessel started, but it's up to you to keep your engine running and move! The words on these pages should motivate you to seek the Word, reflect on God's instructions, and perform what He says. However, nothing will change if you only read this book as a form of entertainment. Additionally, I purposefully vowed to make this and my upcoming books short and sweet. How many unfinished books do you own? I pray this will not be one of them. It is a book you can finish, but first you must begin!

CHAPTER 1
CONFLICT TO TESTIMONY

It is apparent that God creates or allows circumstances to push us to our purpose. We often refer to those circumstances as conflict. Conflict can be external or internal, such as issues at work or struggles in our minds. The supervisor who gives you a hard time, the unplanned layoff or being passed over for a well-deserved promotion are all external variables. Choosing to remain in your current situation -- despite a growing dissatisfaction -- can produce multiple internal struggles and disrupt your mental health. These pressures are common to humanity and will hopefully become catalysts for change. We must remember that God allows conflict to move us from our Safe Place and into our purpose.

Moses is a prime example of the power of conflict; it pushed Moses to his destiny. Prior to exploring his experiences in the Old Testament, it is imperative to review the testimony of God about his servant Moses in the New Testament. Hebrews 11:23-29 reads:

> By faith Moses, when he was born, was hid three months of his parents, because they saw he was a proper child; and they were not afraid of the king's commandment.

> By faith Moses, when he was come to years, refused to be called the son of Pharaoh's daughter;

Choosing rather to suffer affliction with the people of God, than to enjoy the pleasures of sin for a season;

Esteeming the reproach of Christ greater riches than the treasures in Egypt: for he had respect unto the recompense of the reward.

By faith he forsook Egypt, not fearing the wrath of the king: for he endured, as seeing him who is invisible.

Through faith he kept the Passover, and the sprinkling of blood, lest he that destroyed the firstborn should touch them.

By faith they passed through the Red Sea as by dry land: which the Egyptians assaying to do were drowned.

His journey from conflict to testimony included murder, doubt, loneliness, questions, anger, and frustration. Even Moses dealt with sin and struggle on an extreme scale. However, God does not mention any of it. Moses had all the rights and privileges one could have during that time. He lived a luxurious life until he was forced to deal with conflict and, as a result, chose to leave his Safe Place.

We must remember that conflict is not always the enemy's doing. In fact, he has no power, but that which God allows. When God permits an obstacle, we must know its true purpose will work for our good. Sometimes, conflict occurs to strengthen your faith or bring attention to an area in your life that must be adjusted or fine-tuned.

Typically, He has already spoken, revealed, and prompted us to leave the Safe Place, but we insist on remaining content where we are most comfortable. That contentment can be dangerous and at times even deadly. Therefore, conflict becomes a conduit for change.

I remember staying at a job too long. God told me to leave. Two years passed and I did not move my feet. I planned to remain there until retirement and enjoy a six-figure salary, great benefits, and a sizable 401K plan. Realistically speaking, why would I go anywhere?

Additionally, I had a mortgage, children in college along with bills, and everything life brings that requires a check book, debit card number, or a dead president's face.

Although I held onto that job to maintain my way of life, I was miserable. On the inside, I was literally sick, frustrated, and depressed. Yes, me, a spirit-filled, born again believer was miserably comfortable. I knew exactly what I was supposed to do; however, doubt and the trappings of the job prevented me from walking out of the exit door.

Problem after problem continued to arise in the workplace. I recognized the persistent and impending danger in this Safe Place, but I was willing to deal with the problems instead of facing the unknown. The Truth was… I refused to trust God.

At the time, I could not see that Who I knew and what He said was more important than what I could not see or understand. From a natural standpoint, leaving my job was insane. Yet, our nature and natural impulses are not enough to live a fulfilled life through faith. It was "By faith" that Moses pleased God.

The longer I stayed, the greater the conflict became. One day, I decided to just walk away. I showed up, strolled in the Human Resources office, turned in my keys, and resigned. Immediately the weight of the world lifted. I did not have a job lined-up, but I knew God would provide.

Remarkably, I went on quite a few job interviews during the two years it took me to say

"Yes" to God's will. Despite my qualifications, and until I obeyed, every potential employer said "No."

It was not until I moved out of my Safe Place and resigned that I received an offer for a position far beyond my imagination. Soon, business deals that were in limbo began to gain traction. It was as if I had stepped into a new dimension. God was performing what He promised.

Revisiting the Word, Moses, was forced to flee Egypt as a result of conflict. He ended up in Median, by a well, at the perfect place and the perfect time: Kairos!

It is here where Moses meets the daughters of the priest of Median. His actions toward them resulted in a divine connection with Jethro, the priest, who eventually became his father-in-law.

Moses then enters the place of peace, or a Safe Place, but only for a season. He is not forced out this new Safe Place by conflict but is lead through his obedience. Although Moses questioned God, he ultimately fulfilled his assignment as stated in the Book of Hebrews. Generations of God's people are the beneficiaries of Moses' obedience and faith.

What if Moses never fled Egypt? What if he never obeyed the assignment? One of the dangers of the Safe Place is the impact on the lives of others. They are waiting on you to leave the Safe Place.

Chapter 1 Reflection Questions:

1) Are you experiencing internal or external conflict?

2) If yes, why do you think the conflict exists?

3) How long have you been dealing with it?

4) Do you know the solution?

5) Have you spent time in prayer on this matter specifically?

6) What has God said about it?

7) Have you obeyed His instruction?

8) What is your plan of action?

9) Who can you confide in? Plan a time to meet with him, her, or them.

You are leaving your Safe Place!

The Danger of the Safe Place

CHAPTER 2:

THE SAFE PLACE DEFINED

What, where, or who is your Safe Place? According to the Merriam Webster Dictionary (2019), it is "a place intended to be free of bias, conflict, or potentially threatening actions, ideas or conversation."

Can you imagine a world where people are free to be exactly who they want to be without fear of opinions of others? Can you think of a place where you are *not* subjected to stereotypes based on social, economic, racial, or any other superimposed classification? Unfortunately, this freedom from Fear is uncommon. As a result, people decide to conform --

instead of act in opposition -- to the above-mentioned obstacles.

Unfortunately, the most innocent individuals become the most common victims of acquiescence to opinions. Children dare to dream of becoming anything, but well-meaning adults can deter them to more practical pursuits. We place our own biases and stumbling blocks on individuals based on our experiences. We have been taught to respond in fear to the faith-filled dreams of others, especially children:

"You are too short to play that sport."

"You are not smart enough."

"Nobody from here ever made it!"

"It costs too much!"

Certainly, the list of fears and excuses can go on and on. If you listen to those worries, then the world has robbed you of your potential contributions in an area God predestined you to impact. Doubt and discouragement are root reasons why we stay in our

Safe Place.

I remember my middle school math teacher made several negative comments regarding my math skills. I hated her class; it was the longest 55 minutes of the day! It caused me to fear the subject, and I actually dreamed of becoming an engineer! However, I avoided that career field and continue evade mathematics as much as possible. While I am grateful for a career in Human Resources, fear was a factor in my decision-making process because the job did not require extensive arithmetic. I "played it safe" all because of the words of a middle school teacher.

Have you allowed yourself to stay in your Safe Place because of the words or opinions of others? Or, are you "free" and truly walk by faith? If the former is true, then you may have robbed the world of the gift of you! You've handcuffed yourself to your own ideas, doubts, or the dreams other people have for your life.

The reality of a Safe Place varies from person to person based on circumstances, upbringing, or experience. One person's Safe Place can feel like a prison to another. A Safe Place can be as different as ice cream flavors or fashion preferences are from one person to the next. No one is wrong to prefer vanilla over strawberry or a traditional T-shirt over a V-neck. The Safe Place holds the same principles of subjectivity. I abhorred math and felt safe in its absence while another may love numbers and cannot subsist without its presence. One person's Safe Place can feel like a prison to another. However, God knows which place, person, or circumstance is a danger to your destiny.

By definition, it is understandable why one may prefer to stay in his or her Safe Place. By doing so, you create your own utopia: the perfect existence free from biases, conflict and threats. However, is "playing it safe" God's will for your life, the life of a born-again believer? Why would we need faith if it were God's intentions to keep us comfy and cozy in our own ways? We must look beyond the attractiveness of things we can see, know, and understand. It is imperative to answer the call to the unknown just as Abraham did in Hebrew 11:8.

Leaving the Safe Place causes you to enter a dystopia-like existence. It can seem miserable, full of subpar conditions, and may be ridden with struggle. Who wants that? But like a plate full of vegetables before a toddler, it can be just what a growing soul requires.

I remember taking my family on a cruise. When the ship docked in Jamaica, we jumped at the chance to go snorkeling. After receiving the safety gear and basic instructions, we ventured out into the beautiful water to observe the dynamic creatures parading in God's aquarium. I enjoyed snorkeling before, so I knew the drill: just float and enjoy the scenery! However, this time we were close to a few prominent coral reefs.

Out of the blue, a wave threw me against the sharp edges of the reef. I was cut. Blood began streaming from my head and arms like juice from a ripe plum. To add insult to injury, I drifted too far for the others to see or hear me, and I did not want to startle my family by yelling and causing a scene.

Now, I'm a decent swimmer and was adorned in a life vest, but I was also sore and very winded. I had a decision to make: Do I tread water where I was, with the hope that someone sees me, or do I swim toward the shore? I decided to swim the mile in the direction of the shoreline. Well, at least, it looked like a mile. I may not have swam like Michael Phelps, but I moved like I had a mission and nothing could stop me.

At some point the person in charge of the excursion pulled alongside my weary soul and dragged me into the boat's cold embrace. He gave me a reassuring smirk and said, "I saw you struggling."

What if I did not position myself for him to notice me? What if I stayed put, waiting and hoping for a miracle instead of going as far as I could with all the strength I could muster?

God sees our struggle, but we must go as far as we can with what He's given us. We must reposition ourselves for Him to send a boat to carry us the rest of the way. Leaving the Safe Place will leave you a little beat-up, tired and winded, but God will meet you and carry you to the promised land. The truth is He will be with you the whole way.

Unfortunately, if you desire to fulfill the will of God in your life, the Safe Place is not an option for you. In fact, it is probably the antithesis of the definition. The Safe Place is a danger to your health, wealth, and purpose.

Your purpose is the reason God allowed your mother and father to meet and conceive you. It is the space in the world that only you can fill. Yet, when you decide to believe God and move out to fulfill a purpose, prepare to be judged by those who have no clue of who you are or what it took for you to get there. Prepare for some very lonely times and even betrayal. The same people who will pat you on the back may talk behind your back without cause.

Outside of the Safe Place, you may find yourself in the company of new people. You may feel ill-equip to entertain them but remain humble and be strong. It is equally important that you develop the wherewithal to exist in the company of accomplished individuals. Being in their presence can be intimidating but view the experience as an asset -- not an obstacle. Be prepared to add disappointment, loneliness, tears, even doubt and fear to the list of challenges you will face outside of your comfort zone. Let none of them deter you.

Believers are not immune to doubt and fear. We have not found a vaccine for these two most stubborn emotions. Anyone who dares to leave their Safe Place will encounter a moment of trepidation but remember that you face it with the King of Kings by your side.

Our immediate response to a call should be predicated on the Word of God. His Word tells us how big our God is and how small our issues are compared to Him. The Bible reveals the circumstances people faced when they were asked to do the unthinkable.

I personally live by the following scriptures to renew my mind:

"And being fully persuaded that, what he had promised, he was able also to perform." -Romans 4:21

"Now unto him that is able to do exceeding abundantly above all that we ask or think, according to the power that worketh in us..." -Ephesians 3:20

"I can do all things through Christ which strengtheneth me." -Philippians 4:13

It is incumbent to find scriptures that propel you beyond the walls of fear and doubt.

A faith builder can also be song lyrics or poem. One of my favorite poems when facing adversity is "See it Through" by Edgar A. Guest. The first stanza reads:

When you're up against a trouble,
Meet it squarely, face to face;
Lift your chin and set your shoulders,
Plant your feet and take a brace.
When it's vain to try to dodge it,
Do the best that you can do;
You may fail, but you may conquer,
See it through!

However, there is nothing that strengthens me more than God's Word to face a conflict, cruel face, or a challenging place.

The Word is your fuel and weapon in conflict. When you feel the weight of fear, faith is your shield and umbrella. Do not attempt to leave a Safe Place without the whole armor of God according to Ephesians 6:10-18. We fail only when we stay in Safe

Place based on our own ego and personal will. With God, we cannot lose.

Prepare for the journey in the Word. You will conquer if you follow His step by step directions. God will not send you on a mission into unfamiliar territory without a plan. Seek His face and find wisdom in the Word. Put your favorite song of encouragement on repeat and go forth, swim with all your might, and trust in the Father like He knows exactly what He's doing.

Chapter 2 Reflection Questions:

1)   What is your Safe Place?

2)   What keeps you there?

3)   Who or what do you need to confront in order to
leave?

4)   What scriptures, songs, or poems, can give you
strength for the journey?

Remember what God had done for you before and allow that to fuel you.

You are leaving your Safe Place!

CHAPTER 3:

SAFETY NETS KILL PROMISES

What are you expecting from God? If you ask believers what they want from God, while on Earth, many will say His Promises or His will. God agrees with that very desire according to 2 Corinthians 1:20 that states, "For all the promises of God in him are yea, and in him Amen, unto the glory of God by us."

Unfortunately, chances are that you will not obtain those promises in a Safe Place. The 13th chapter of the Book of Numbers tells the story of Moses obeying the Lord's instruction to send men to search the land of Canaan. Canaan was the land filled with all the prosperity that God promised His people. In fact, the Lord said in verse two: "Send thou men, that they may search the land of Canaan, *which I give unto the children* of Israel." Therefore, the land was theirs before they even set foot in the place!

Moses sent spies to Canaan to include Joshua and Caleb, and they returned with a favorable report. Both men witnessed and testified about the prosperity and promise of the place. However, ten other Hebrews returned with a report filled with fear; they complained about all the potential challenges and obstacles in Canaan. Their faithless testimony permeated with the people of Israel so much that they cried real tears and made plans to return to Egypt. Their place of bondage seemed safer than the prospect of receiving the promise of God in an unfamiliar place.

There are several takeaways from this event. It is to remind us to only focus what God has shown you and believe what He said – not what you see. The other stuff is His to handle. When you decide to leave the Safe Place, it is imperative to remind yourself to

walk by faith and not by sight (2 Corinthians 5:7).
When you leave the Safe Place, the giants may look
insurmountable, but OUR God is bigger. Even after
all the miraculous feats God performed to save them
from it, Egypt was more desirable to the children of
Israel. The Safe Place does not mean a good place. It is
just a place of familiarity.

Have you ever driven your car with the engine
light on for an extended time? In fact, you get used to
it. The engine light is a clear indication that something
is wrong. Eventually, you have the vehicle serviced and
the light goes out. Ironically, and for some crazy
reason, you miss the light! That is what Egypt was to
the children of Israel. They had become accustomed to
functioning in miserable conditions; it became their
Safe Place. Even with the many dangers therein, some
Israelites wanted to go back and dwell as slaves.

Despite the temptation, never look back to go
back. Lot's wife suffered greatly from looking back.
When you truly read the narrative of Sodom and

Gomorrah, you would assume she should have been the first one ready to go! However, something made her disobey God's instructions, resulting in her transformation into a pillar of salt (Genesis 19:26).

I highly doubt God will turn anyone else into a salt pile anytime soon, but we can become pillars in our Safe Places. We can be so firm or rigid that we become immovable and a support for the Safe Place. We should leave, but we enable our own inability to move with God's command. Relationships, jobs, or even places of worship can become that place. The engine light is clearly on, but we are used to it and comfortable, so we stay. It can be difficult, but do not look back and retreat!

The enemy will attempt to make you miss the past, but we must rehearse Philippians 13-14:

> Brethren, I count not myself to have apprehended: but this one thing I do, forgetting those things which are behind, and

reaching forth unto those things which are before, I press toward the mark for the prize of the high calling of God in Christ Jesus.

When you recognize the Danger of the Safe Place and refuse to look back to go back, you are that much closer to the manifestation of God's Promises in your life.

Chapter 3 Reflections Questions:

1) In what areas of your life are you looking back? Why?

2) What areas in your life do you feel are at a standstill? Why?

3) Have you suffered from looking back or standing still?

4) Who has your decision(s) impacted?

5) Are you ready to move forward?

6) What area of your life will you address first? Develop a plan!

You are leaving your Safe Place!

The Danger of the Safe Place

CHAPTER 4:

A DANGEROUS MIND

The Safe Place is not relegated to physical changes or actions. It is equally dangerous to have safe mindsets and customs. Peter's experience in Acts 10:9-16 is a great example:

> On the morrow, as they went on their journey, and drew nigh unto the city, Peter went up upon the housetop to pray about the sixth hour:
>
> And he became very hungry, and would have eaten: but while they made ready, he fell into a trance,

And saw heaven opened, and a certain vessel descending unto him, as it had been a great sheet knit at the four corners, and let down to the earth:

Wherein were all manner of four-footed beasts of the earth, and wild beasts, and creeping things, and fowls of the air.

And there came a voice to him, Rise, Peter; kill, and eat.

But Peter said, Not so, Lord; for I have never eaten anything that is common or unclean.

And the voice *spake* unto him again the second time, What God hath cleansed, *that* call not thou common.

This was done thrice: and the vessel was received up again into heaven.

In this passage, Peter actually responds "not so" --also known as "No" -- to God's instruction to eat. He avoided eating such things his entire life, and even a vision from heaven and the voice of God Himself couldn't shake his ways. Peter ultimately understands the vision, but how many of us have turned customs into pillars? How many of us have turned traditions or practices into pillars that even God cannot shift?

Mind pillars can manifest in several ways, such as staying in dead churches, working a 9-5 that you do not enjoy, avoiding new relationships, or not completing your educational pursuits. What you choose to do in honor of tradition is a mind pillar if God specifically told you to do something different. Even if your entire family tree attended the same church since the American Civil War, you must shift if God says move. In our culture, you can even have reservations about meeting people who do not look like you or worship like you. The list could go on. Subsequently, Safe Place dangers start with the mind. Many times, mind pillars are a result of groupthink: forced values and thought processes, which are often a result of our cultural standards and implicit biases.

I almost fell victim to a mind pillar, which could have cost my youngest son an amazing opportunity. He was in the sixth grade when he came home from school one day and asked permission to play lacrosse. I knew nothing about the game. In fact, I never really knew any African Americans who played it, and I didn't care to see people running up and down the field with sticks! Boy was I wrong! My son picked up the game very quickly and became really good. He played in high school and was offered an opportunity to play at the collegiate level.

Although he chose to play college football, my love for the game continues. Not only did I learn that the sport was more than just people running up and down the field with sticks, I met and became friends with people who did not look like me, found out the rich history of the game, and discovered that many African-Americans have played the sport at a high level. In fact, I now encourage parents to let their children play lacrosse. Don't allow groupthink to become mind pillars and rob you and your seed of rich experiences.

Meanwhile, can you imagine the inner turmoil Saul encountered before his conversion to the great Apostle Paul? His very existence was predicated on his reputation for persecution of Christians. Acts 9:1-5 says,

> And Saul, yet breathing out threatenings and slaughter against the disciples of the Lord, went unto the high priest, And desired of him letters to Damascus to the synagogues, that if he found any of this way, whether they were men or women, he might bring them bound unto Jerusalem. And as he journeyed, he came near Damascus: and suddenly there shined round about him a light from heaven: And he fell to the earth, and heard a voice saying unto him, Saul, Saul, why persecutest thou me? And he said, Who art thou, Lord? And the Lord

said, I am Jesus whom thou persecutest: it is
hard for thee to kick against the pricks.

Paul was a killer of Christians who found God.
How could he become like the very people whom he
sought to persecute? How long did he battle internally?
Why did God have to go to such an extreme to make
Saul convert? God told Paul that he was "kick[ing]
against the pricks." In other words, Paul was only
hurting himself by fighting against the almighty One.
Paul's life and soul were in grave danger because his
Safe Place went against God and His people.
Essentially, staying in any Safe Place is a decision to go
against God.

When you make up your mind to leave the
Safe Place, everything you were could change and
people will try to handcuff you to your past. Saul faced
the same scrutiny. Together, Saul and his cohorts
hunted and killed those who believed in Jesus. Then,
virtually overnight, those same peers witnessed Saul's
newfound devotion to Jesus as Savior and Lord! Paul,

formerly known as Saul, transformed from the hunter to the hunted. Could you imagine the weight of his reputation on his new life? Saul was an assassin with the respect of his murdering peers. Suddenly, his name changed, and his loyalty performed an about face. It certainly showed people the power of God. Many times, we attempt to carry on as the old us because we fear what others will think and what they may do. God changed Saul into Paul as an extreme example of His grace, mercy, and power to make us a new creature.

As new creatures, we know that we are not the same and truly want to leave the Safe Place, but we may also wrestle with thoughts such as "what will they say?" However, if you're bold enough to leave the Safe Place, you must be bold enough to stand tall in your new place of faith. You may have to stand alone and without the approval of your former entourage. Paul certainly could not straddle the fence; he lost his 'killer card' and everything he knew. He laid down his life on earth to go with the God of heaven and earth.

After a shift, we sometimes want to relate to people or show an overly humble persona to remain the same in the eyes of familiar faces. Please understand that humility *is* vital to Believers. However, being humble to please people, because you fear what they think, will cause you grief when God wants to manifest His promises in your life. I remember taking a significant position within the local government. As excited as I was, I did not openly announce the title for several reasons. Most had to do with a flawed internal mindset. I was afraid of negative feedback and often thought, "what if I fail?"

These degenerative ideas ran through my mind for an entire month into the position. They were triggered by issues I had experienced with a previous employer. I looked back mentally and allowed my fear to damper what should have been an exciting time. Eventually, I overcame the mental challenges, but I robbed myself of what should have been a great experience from the start.

Mindsets matter when you leave your Safe Place. It could take some time to overcome the mental roadblocks. Remember Romans 12:2:

"And be not conformed to this world: but be ye transformed by the renewing of your mind, that ye may prove what is that good, and acceptable, and perfect, will of God."

When you decide to walk out on faith the enemy will attack your mind to keep you in a Safe Place and out of the will of God. What you *think* is safe can endanger your destiny. We please the Father with our faith, not with our ability to tuck ourselves away in our own will.

Chapter 4 Reflection Questions:

1) In what area(s) has God challenged you?

2) How has he pricked your heart regarding those areas?

3) What effects can you directly relate to not responding to His pricks?

4) Do you fear your identity may change?

5) What about your current identity is important to you?

6) Why do you think God is challenging you to change evolve?

7) Are you ready?

You are leaving your Safe Place!

CHAPTER 5:

ALL IN LIKE HIM

Jesus left heaven for you. The end!

I could have started and ended the book with that one sentence. Our Lord and Savior left the safest place in all eternity to accomplish the will of God, to reclaim us to Himself. His earthly ministry was no different.

Jesus never "played it safe!" By age twelve, Jesus challenged the Scribes and Pharisees instead of walking safely alongside Joseph and Mary. Later in life, He walked on water. He defied all norms of thinking, societal practices, and even religion itself. Jesus even knowingly went places that jeopardized his physical safety and His reputation.

The following is a short list of how Jesus denied the Safe Place on Earth:

❖ Performed miracles on the Sabbath

❖ Sat with sinners

❖ Selected disciples who were not considered religious leaders, including one who would betray him

❖ Went to the mountain to be tempted by satan

❖ Endured the cross

This chapter could fill this entire book. In fact, John 21:25 (NIV), says "Jesus did many other things as well. If every one of them were written down, I suppose that even the whole world would not have room for the books that would be written."

Imagine, then believe, that the same resurrection power that raised Him from the dead dwells within us. We are filled with the person of the Holy Spirit. As such, we can fulfill God's purpose in our lives.

That purpose is not completed by staying in safe places, either mental or physical. When we confine ourselves to a Safe Place, we handcuff our life to what we see in the natural -- instead of what He said. We embrace limitations placed on us by people and systems instead of what God said was possible.

As I pen this chapter, I am challenged in the Spirit to not settle. This is not it! There is more He wants me to do as an author and businessman. I am telling you what He is telling me, DON'T DROP the ANCHOR!

I absolutely hate when I have time to watch television and suddenly the most annoying sound blares with a voice: "We interrupt this program to bring you a special announcement." Those responsible for the interruption couldn't care less about what you were watching or where you were in the program because the interruption must take place. I declare to you that God is about to interrupt your program!

Prepare to move from your Safe Place. I am telling you from experience, there is no need to resist the unction God has placed in you. Trust Him and know the safest place you can be is in His will. Your purpose and promises are waiting for you to let go of the Safe Place. Any place without God is the most dangerous place on earth.

Guest Testimony:

Do What God Says

In the following excerpt from his personal story of victory Lloyd Wheatley offers a definitive testimony of defying the Safe Place and going with God. For ... [We] overcame him [our enemy] by the blood of the Lamb, and by the word of [our] testimony..." (Revelation 12:11).

In July of 1994, I had achieved my goal of working for Corporate America and providing for my family. Life was good, but it wasn't great because it didn't feel like my best.

I fantasized about having my own business and being the boss. This never materialized because of a fear of limited finances to accommodate our daily cost of living.

My wife had her dreams and ambitions too. I will paraphrase what is written that "He that has found a wife has found a good thing." Don't get this twisted, I was not the sole driving force behind our family's decisions. The crazy part of this is we were not church going people at the time.

God strategically delayed the desires of my heart until I came to know HIM and trust HIM and lean on HIM. Then and only then did HE allow me to begin to walk in my destiny. To do so before I confessed HIM as LORD would have been a disaster.

The single most prolific instruction that stood out for me in his Book is "DO NOT FEAR." It appears approximately 93 times with variations of "Do NOT BE AFRAID" approximately 103 times in the Bible. So, why are believers still afraid after GOD told us the opposite over and over again? It's simple, we are not perfect like HIM. We are simply moving in the direction of perfection until we see Him face to face.

Once I was able to focus on HIS Word, I was able to and lose my ego. Then I could follow His will. The first thing I had to do was leave my job. God – and my understanding of business and finances -- gave me foresight on the future of my position. My so-called secure job was in danger of elimination. Also, I hated answering to another man who had bad intentions. The Baltimore city kid in me wanted to step out and handle the situation. Old school me said, "take him out." THATS right, "kick his natural ..." You understand. Somehow, by the grace of God, my former ways were suppressed. I left that job and started toward my destiny.

Later that same year, I started a company in transportation after a relative made an informal comment about the low cost of limousines in Baltimore. After twenty-five years, several millions of dollars was the result of that comment. What's fascinating was making something from nothing. The company only existed in my mind. No one else could see it, and I could only explain it to a point. When I tried to talk about it, I noticed that not too many people seemed fired up and ready to jump in.

Well yeah, I soon began to experience feelings of doubt, until it hit me: DO NOT FEAR! God's message was clear:

> Your dream is bigger than your fear and by the way, no one is going to be more excited than you are with your own dream, not even your spouse. They will be supportive out of love, but don't be discouraged if they do not jump in with both feet.

GOD was right. I had a learning curve to surmount. Then, He sent the right people and opened doors for us to prosper. Yes, I was at the helm of a prosperous ship, and God was our wind. Together, my family and I shared an abundant life.

I was able to provide for other families by paying wages, giving money for family and friends to go to college, and lending to support home ownership.

We were even able to provide funds to a stranger to help bury her mother. My wife and I happened to be in the right place at the right time. It wasn't much to me, but it was more than what the government provided as final expenses. It was GOD allowing me to fulfill my purpose. This was different. I really felt good helping others.

The story continues in the year 2000; theY2K craze had come and gone. Six years elapsed since I had begun my business, and things were not going so well. With all my best efforts we were just breaking even. It looked like my big change came and was on its way out. I remember thinking, "I better quit this business and get a job," but also wondering, "How I'm I going to pay back all the debt I created so far?"

We had car loans, utility bills, credit cards and -- oh yeah -- the basics like food to consider! We had no extra money in the bank. Then it happened, a voice said, "You are not in the limousine business, you are in the Transportation business. Limousine service is a market! You can do anything in the business."

This wisdom changed my mindset. Fast forward in the same year, I applied for a state transportation bid and won! I also decided it was the perfect time to stay safe in my current lane and flirt with the FEAR again. I preferred to hold tight to the "burning rope" I knew versus the unfamiliar next step. My excuses were great: 1) The bid was too involved; 2) You needed investment capital for new equipment, and 3) A myriad of things had to be in place just three months from approval. Oh well, "this ain't me" I thought.

I threw the bid away in the trash and walked away. More excuses took over: 4) It's too much for me to do, 5) I'm broke anyway and just barely making it, and 6) I'm not going into more debt. "Not right now!", I said. The excuses rang louder than my faith: Hypocrisy! I tied both hands behind my back by doing nothing. This was open disobedience to the word GOD gave me.

Then the seventh year of business began. It was 2007, and the bid is back on my desk again because no one else in the state put in for it. The GOD of a second chance made it possible for me to try it again and sent the right people to nourish His plan.

Earlier in the year, I attended an entrepreneurial forum at a local community college and met a person named Leah. Her husband, Kenny, wrote a book on the dangers of credit card use. This was extremely interesting because I had also written a book -- as a side hobby-- about a western fictional character. Coincidently, her husband and I used the same publishing company. The company was a rip off and took us to the cleaners, as a manner of speaking. I eventually met her husband, Kenny, in Philadelphia at a Minority Business Chamber of Commerce luncheon. Little did I know that GOD was setting me up to succeed.

Yet, after all the planning for the bid, I still did not have any money to invest. I agonized over the thought for three days. Finally, I decided to look to someONE beyond my understanding. Sitting at my desk in our basement, I asked out loud for GOD's help. I had exhausted all of my ability and came to the end of myself. I had nothing left, my mind was as dark as the room around me. A voice said clearly "CALL KENNY."

I immediately thought, "I can't call him and ask him for money??? I hardly know the man. We only met once. That's crazy!"

Wait a minute, "DO NOT BE AFRAID" is what my faith replied to my fears!

I called Kenny. He then provided all the down payment for the bond to the insurance underwriter and used his personal corporate FED-EX account to overnight the package from Pennsylvania to Dover, Delaware to complete the bid. Kenny is a saved believer also. His lack of hesitation set a high example of what I am supposed to do as a man of God. I had a credible example of Christianity performing right before my eyes. He didn't even go to my church nor live in my neighborhood or county… Imagine that?

I prayed to God: "If you allow me to get this bid, I will raise you before all men and will be a servant unto you for the rest of my days."

How ridiculous and pathetic was that! I tried to tell GOD what He will have to do to get me on his side. WARNING!!! Be careful bargaining with GOD. He will test you.

I got the bid. It started out being four times what my salary was in my last corporate job. This bid was on top of the business income I already had. I still needed to get the equipment. When I told my mentor about my obstacles, he drove me to Exton, Pennsylvania to get a brand-new cutaway bus for a zero-interest loan of $5k. The repayment plan was heaven-sent; virtually I could pay him what and when I could. His exact words to me than was "I know that you will pay it back. I am not worried."

WHHHAAAAT? He did not "play it safe" with me. He listened to God's prompting and blessed me and a caravan behind me. Yet another credible man was giving through faith right in front of my eyes. The gift of giving and not expecting anything. WOW! I was impressed; sign me up for this camp. My mentor has since transitioned to be with the Father, but I was able to learn valuable lessons from his life.

My wife, Kenny, and my mentor all weighed in on GOD's promise to me and kept pushing me toward my destiny. I soon had a new home built, sold my old home in record time, helped my kid through college, and, before long, my wife retired 10 years early at 50. We paid off all my debts.

Eventually, I began to grow complacent and downright lazy in my faith walk, AGAIN. I was in a NEW SAFE PLACE in the form of wealth and prosperity that I had not experienced before. With significant cash in the bank, I felt I could go the way I wanted. The storms passed over the years; I kept my end of the bargain. But GOD was saying come closer to learn more of me and more about you!

It was 2009. The first African American
President was elected into office, but there was a bit of
foulness in the financial world's air. Little did anyone
know how bad the smell was going to be that January.
Ultimately, America's financial collapsed. The funding
for my lucrative contract stopped. Drivers were laid
off, revenue was gone, no cash reserves remained in
the bank, and business was falling. The end was near.

As I sat at my office desk on the highway, I
considered all the things I knew technically. I had
grown very knowledgeable in business and had
overcome a multitude of problems previously. "There
is always something that can be done," I thought to
myself.

God had given me the experience, education,
and wherewithal to figure it out. Well, as things got
worst with lenders, I also thought, "Just shut it down
and file bankruptcy to protect what's left."

Banks were calling for payments on vehicles,
the mortgage, tax deposits, and credit card. However,

it didn't stop there. I had no money to live. I couldn't pay the mortgage on our primary residence. My wife left her job early and deferred her pension until her 60 & 62 birthday, which wouldn't be for another six to eight years. Utilities, food, gas, insurance, and health care were pressing needs and all my credit cards were maxed out.

I continued to work most of the time, but I could not pay my drivers. Several my team members retired, and I understood. A couple workers stayed to help and did not care how much we paid them; they were content to just be there. There finally came a time when I could hardly afford to pay the mortgage on our primary residence. Then, a distant friend, who lived in a different state and was also laid off and unemployed, stepped in and paid our mortgage of $1600.00.

During this financial crisis, everybody was in the same boat. This was bigger than you. Many businesses were struggling. The stock market was in the eights. It was reported that some people committed suicide due to financial ruins. That's how powerful the consequences of failure can be. I get it, and that's why I say it's not easy being the boss. It's takes a lot of guts and prayer.

How were we going to make it? The voice spelled out specific instructions of what to do and who to call. BUT NOW, I didn't think about it I just DID IT! A secondary lending organization called First State Community Loan Fund did what no other bank would. I used them in my earlier years in the business, and because of our favorable history, they consolidated our business equipment and credit cards into one loan collateralized by the business property. I still had to be the guarantor for the loan. The consolidation loan went through for $90k at slightly higher than normal interest rate. We are back in business and given a chance to survive.

It is now 2019 and all but $17k has been paid back. All the vehicle titles are clear; meanwhile, new vehicles have been purchased. Cash reserves are back, and savings are up over 652%. We are on a record pace. There is MORE! My wife now has three pension incomes; our resident payoff is accelerated with a few years to pay off. I also receive social security as an added income; however, it is not needed as a means for day to day living. I'm saving more in real money, GOLD, which I never had before. We were able to weather the storm over the past ten years.

God continually blessed me through all my suffering. I was able to repay the friend who paid our mortgage and saved us from the bank. When I tried to give it back, they refused the money and told me it was up to me to continue to bless others by passing on the blessing. I did just that and have never stopped giving. I do these things now because I can discern who's serious and who are true believers. HE has quickened my spirit and suppressed my soul and my Ego.

HE has made me the TEACHER in his fivefold ministry. It was my destiny to be so. I don't even have to think about the money or the business as before anymore. Yes, it's important, but I know God will continue to provide as always. I know that now. I just teach whenever and wherever I can on the lessons of my life. GOD provides the security and everything else in my life. It's seems almost too easy to trust Him.

This can be confusing to the casual observer as I may seem egotistical instead of just confident. My lack of fear can seem hard or unsympathetic to others. Again, not true. I do not believe in a no-win scenario if I have GOD on my side. The experiences a believer encounters may not be pretty, glamorous or sexy, but it is always effective in the end. Who cares what people think?

I say this with a forced conviction and attitude when I say to anyone, DON'T THINK ABOUT IT, JUST DO IT! Do what He says! You will win.

Disclaimer: Don't be Careless!!!

I hope the previous pages inspired you to reflect on your current status and inspired you to leave your Safe Place. However, it is not a pass to be careless like Icarus. The story of Icarus is Greek mythology in which a son didn't heed to his father's instructions.

In short, Icarus is the son of Daedalus. King Minos decided to imprison Dedalus and his family, including Icarus. Daedalus carefully crafts wings for them to escape, but they are made from wax. He warns Icarus not to fly close to the sun. Of course, his son did not listen. Ultimately the sun melted the wax and Icarus fell to a tragic death.

Similarly, there are several warnings issued before a loving parent finally allows their child to cross the street alone. "Look both ways", "use the crosswalk," "run" and so on. God's has a list of warnings as well. We must appropriately apply our faith and heed to the warnings God has given us.

Luke 4:1-12 tells the story of the Devil taking Jesus to a high mountain and tempting Him. One of those temptations was the challenge to jump from the mountain since he was the Son of God. The devil even relied on the Word to support his challenge. Of course, Jesus responds appropriately, "thou shall not tempt the Lord thy God."

As you prepare to leave your Safe Place remember to apply your faith appropriately. There are still instructions -- both natural and spiritual – to follow. Listen to the daily directions God will provide along the way. Of course, He will speak to Himself. He will use natural rules and instructions to lead and guide you through this most amazing time of your life.

As I conclude my very first, book I am filled with excitement. By faith, I believe you have decided to join me in leaving your Safe Place.

Congratulations!

What's your Safe Place story?

Join the conversation by sharing your story at
www.Dangerofsafeplace.wixsite.com or on
Facebook: The Danger Of The Safe Place: BOOK Release
https://www.facebook.com/TheDangerOfTheSafePlace/.